Baby Whale Rescue
The True Story of J.J.

Caroline Arnold
and Richard Hewett

W9-ATJ-908

Troll

BridgeWater Paperback

We are grateful to SeaWorld of California in San Diego for its generous support and cooperation with us on this project. In particular, we thank the Department of Public Relations; Robert Couey and Ken Bohn in the Department of Photo Services; Dr. Ann Bowles and Dr. Brent Stewart at the Hubbs–SeaWorld Research Institute; and Dr. Jim McBain and all of the animal-care specialists who worked with J.J. and helped us get to know her. We also thank Dr. Jenifer Hurley from the Moss Landing Marine Lab in Moss Landing, California; the sea lions, Beaver and Sake; and Jasper Sircus. J.J. was named after Judi Jones, the former director of Friends of the Sea Lion in Laguna Beach, California, as a memorial to her work with sea mammals. Judi Jones died of cancer in January 1997. J.J. was returned to the sea by the U.S. Coast Guard cutter *Conifer* from the U.S. Naval Station in San Diego. J.J. is now under the supervision of the National Marine Fisheries Service, whose staff will watch for her as they monitor gray whales in the Pacific.

Photo credits: Richard Hewett, pages 3, 6, 11, 12, 14, 15, 19, 20, 22, 23, 24; Katy Penland, page 5; SeaWorld of California Department of Photography: Ken Bohn, front cover, back cover, and pages 1, 7, 9, 10, 13, 16, 17, 18, 21, 25, 32; Robert Couey, pages 8, 26, 27, 28, 29, 30, 31; Candice Lenney, page 4.

Text copyright © 1999 by Caroline Arnold.

Published by BridgeWater Paperback, an imprint and trademark of Troll Communications L.L.C.

All rights reserved. No part of this book may be reproduced or utilized in any form or by any means, electronic or mechanical, including photocopying, recording, or by any information storage and retrieval system, without written permission from the publisher.

Published in hardcover by BridgeWater Books.

Printed in the United States of America.

10 9 8 7 6 5 4 3 2 1

Library of Congress Cataloging-in-Publication Data

Arnold, Caroline.
    Baby whale rescue: the true story of J.J. / by Caroline Arnold and Richard Hewett.
        p.   cm.
    Summary: Describes how J.J., a baby gray whale born off the California coast and separated from her mother, was rescued and returned to the open sea.
        ISBN 0-8167-4961-2 (lib. bdg.)   ISBN 0-8167-5653-8 (pbk.)
    1. Gray whale—California—San Diego—Biography—Juvenile literature. 2. Wildlife rescue—California—San Diego—Juvenile literature. 3. SeaWorld—Juvenile literature. [1. Gray whale. 2. Whales. 3. Wildlife rescue.] I. Hewett, Richard. II. Title.
QL737.C425A75 1999
599.5′22′0929—dc21   98-31229

You can learn more about J.J. by visiting the SeaWorld web site at www.seaworld.org

INTRODUCTION

Gray whales live in the Pacific Ocean and spend the summer months off the coast of Alaska. When winter comes, they swim south to warmer waters near Baja California, which is part of Mexico. There, in shallow lagoons, female gray whales give birth to their babies. Sometimes a baby whale is born before its mother reaches Mexico. Occasionally these newborn whales and their mothers become separated. Without its mother, a baby whale cannot survive. J.J. was a baby whale who was born somewhere off the California coast during the winter gray-whale migration and soon became separated from her mother. She was discovered on January 10, 1997, at the Marina del Rey beach in Los Angeles, California. The young whale was exhausted, hungry, and near death. This is the story of J.J.'s rescue, recovery, and return to the sea.

It was a cold, windy day in January 1997. At a beach in southern California, storm clouds hung over the horizon and waves crashed onto the sand. People walking along the shore noticed a large, dark animal rolling in the surf. When it turned, they could see huge flippers and a massive flat tail. The animal was a 14-foot-long baby gray whale!

This baby whale, or calf, was a young female. She was so weak she could barely move. She needed help soon. Dozens of people, including lifeguards, police, and animal-rescue volunteers, got the baby whale out of the water and onto a truck. Rescuers decided to take her to SeaWorld in San Diego. There, experts could give her food, water, and the care she needed. Later,

when the whale was healthy and old enough to be on her own, they would return her to the ocean. But first she had to grow strong.

At SeaWorld, caretakers put the baby whale in a shallow pool and held her steady. They made sure that the top of her head stayed out of the water so she could breathe. A whale, just like other mammals, needs to breathe air. The air goes into the whale's lungs through openings in the head called blowholes. When the whale blows out, moisture in the breath forms a misty spout.

When veterinarians examined the baby whale, they decided she was about a week old. They could tell she had not had anything to eat or drink for several days. She needed food and water right away.

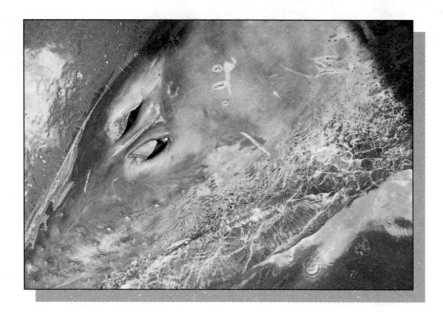

Normally, a whale calf gets all the food and water it needs from its mother's milk. Caretakers did not have whale milk to feed the baby, so they made a special formula by mixing together water, dry milk, whipping cream, ground herring, and other nutrients. At first they poured the thick liquid through a long tube directly into the whale's stomach. Soon the calf was able to drink it by herself. With regular feedings, she began to gain strength and grow.

During the baby whale's first days at SeaWorld, caretakers kept watch over her day and night. They wanted to give her a name. They decided to call the calf J.J. after their friend Judi Jones, who had cared for many stranded sea mammals.

On the day that J.J. was rescued, she weighed only 1,670 pounds. That is huge compared with the weight of a human baby, but tiny for a gray whale. Gray whales are among the giants of the ocean. An adult can be more than 50 feet long and weigh up to 70,000 pounds. That's as heavy as ten elephants!

By the time J.J. had been at SeaWorld for a month, she had gained 900 pounds. She had also grown 18 inches in length. J.J. no longer fit in her small pool. Her caretakers decided to move her to a large pool next to Shamu Stadium.

Moving a 2,500-pound animal is not easy. J.J. was placed in a sling, lifted out of her pool with a crane, and taken to her new home.

At J.J.'s new pool, visitors could see her above water and look through a large window to see her underwater as well. In many ways, she looked like a small, living submarine.

J.J. was curious about her surroundings and seemed to enjoy exploring. Propelling herself with her tail flukes, she glided through the water in graceful slow motion. Large flippers on the sides of her body helped her swim.

Visitors loved watching J.J., and she became one of the most popular animals at SeaWorld. News of her rescue and recovery had made her famous around the world. People who couldn't visit J.J. in person could learn about her at the SeaWorld web site on the Internet.

When J.J. was four months old, she began to eat squid, small fish, and other solid foods. One of her favorite foods was krill, a kind of small shellfish. J.J. learned that if she opened her mouth when one of her caretakers came to the side of her pool, she would usually get something to eat.

For several months, J.J. was fed both solid food and her special milk formula, but by the time she was eight months old, she no longer needed milk and ate only solid foods. Like all growing youngsters, J.J. had a big appetite. She sometimes ate as much as 500 pounds of food a day!

J.J. is the first baby gray whale ever rescued and cared for at a marine park. Her stay at SeaWorld gave people a rare chance to learn about gray whales and to see one up close.

Like other gray whales, J.J. has no teeth. Instead, she has a stiff, brush-like fringe, called baleen, around the upper sides of her mouth. A gray whale usually feeds by sucking food off the ocean floor through the side of its mouth. Then it uses its large tongue to push water and mud out of its mouth through the baleen. The baleen works as a strainer to catch the pieces of food, which the whale then swallows.

When J.J. returned to the ocean, no people would be there to feed her. She would have to find her own food. Her caretakers began to place some of her food on the bottom of her pool. J.J. quickly learned to locate the food and suck it up. Each day, divers put the food in a different place so that J.J. would have practice searching for it. Then, the next morning, when J.J.'s pool was cleaned, the leftover food was weighed. By subtracting that amount from the total amount J.J. had been given, her caretakers knew exactly how much she had eaten.

As J.J. got older, the layer of fat under her skin grew thicker. This fat, or blubber, would provide energy during her first weeks at sea. It would also help keep her warm.

While J.J. was learning how to feed herself, her caretakers started planning her return to the sea. They decided that the best time to release her would be in the early spring. At that time of year, groups of gray whales would be swimming past southern California on their way north to their summer feeding grounds in Alaska. J.J.'s caretakers hoped she would join one of the groups.

Gray whales "talk" to each other underwater by making loud sounds. Scientists at SeaWorld played recordings of gray whales for J.J. so she could become familiar with the calls. They also listened to J.J. to make sure she knew how to make her own gray-whale sounds.

In January, shortly after J.J.'s first birthday, she was joined in her pool for several hours each day by two sea lions. Scientists were training the sea lions to swim underwater with videocameras on their backs. When the sea lions are in the water, the cameras automatically record whatever is in front of them. Scientists expect to learn more about whales and other ocean animals from video pictures taken by these trained sea lions.

The sea lions' practice sessions with J.J. helped them get used to being close to whales. At the same time, they gave J.J. the chance to meet other animals, just as she would when she went back to the ocean.

By the end of February, J.J. weighed more than 18,000 pounds and was nearly 30 feet long. Soon it would be time for her to go back to the ocean.

J.J.'s caretakers began the final preparations for her release. They practiced putting her in the sling that would lift her out of the pool. They made sure she would fit into the truck that would take her to the harbor. They rehearsed each step of the plan over and over.

Everyone was wondering what J.J. would do after she was put into the sea. On the day of her release, four small radio transmitters would be fastened onto J.J.'s back. Once J.J. was in the ocean, signals from the transmitters would be detected each time she came to the surface of the

water to breathe. They would tell people where she was and the direction in which she was going.

Finally, the day of J.J.'s release arrived—Tuesday, March 31, 1998. Everyone who had taken care of J.J. was both happy and sad to see her go. They had worked hard getting her ready for life in the ocean. They would miss her, but they knew she belonged in the sea.

Early that morning, the SeaWorld staff lifted J.J. out of her pool for the last time. Held safely in her red sling, J.J. was placed in a container on the back of a large truck. Inside the container, a foam lining made a soft bed where she could rest while she was transported to the harbor. During the short trip, J.J.'s caretakers stayed with her to make sure she was calm and comfortable.

Under a cloudy morning sky, the truck carrying J.J. made its way through the streets of San Diego. When it arrived at the harbor, J.J. was lifted out of the container and onto a Coast Guard ship. Normally, the ship's large crane is used to hoist heavy buoys and put them into the ocean. This day, the crew would use it to lower a 10-ton whale into the water!

The crew fastened J.J. and her sling to the deck of the boat. As they worked, they sprayed water over J.J.'s back to keep her skin cool and moist.

Then everything was checked once more to make sure J.J. was secure. At last, the boat sailed out of the harbor.

The ship stopped when it was about two miles out from land. At last, the moment for J.J.'s return to the sea had arrived. The crew swung the sling over the side of the ship and lowered J.J. to the ocean surface. "Release the whale!" shouted the captain. One side of the sling dropped, and J.J. slipped into the water. After fourteen months at SeaWorld, she was back home again. Everyone cheered as J.J. took a big breath, dove deep, and disappeared. The young whale was on her own.

During the next few days, scientists patrolled the area in a small boat. They watched and listened for J.J. Several times they saw her poke her head up to look around. The beeps of her radio transmitter showed that

she was moving about and exploring. It seemed as if J.J. was behaving like a normal, wild gray whale.

Scientists had hoped that J.J.'s radio transmitters would allow them to follow her movements for several months. But by the end of the young whale's second day at sea, all her transmitters had fallen off. The last signal showed that she was heading north, like other gray whales on their way to Alaska.

Life in the ocean will not be easy. J.J. will have to find food, stay healthy, and avoid danger. But with luck, she will grow up, lead a long life, and make many trips along the California coast. And each winter and spring, as gray whales pass by on their annual migration, we will wonder if one

of them might be J.J., the baby whale who went back to the sea.